Adoption

by

W.B. Godbey

First Fruits Press
Wilmore,
Kentucky
c2017

Adoption.
By W.B. Godbey.
First Fruits Press, © 2017

ISBN: 9781621717157 (print), 9781621717164 (digital), 9781621717171 (kindle)

Digital version at http://place.asburyseminary.edu/godbey/3/

Godbey, W. B. (William Baxter), 1833-1920.
 Adoption / by W.B. Godbey. – Wilmore, KY : First Fruits Press, ©2017.
  36 pages ; cm.
  Reprint. Previously published: Greensboro, North Carolina. : Apostolic Messenger Office, [190-?].
  ISBN: 9781621717157 (pbk.)
  1. Children of God--Biblical Teaching. 2. Adoption--Religious aspects--Biblical teaching. 3. Bible. Romans VIII, 16-17—Criticism, interpretation, etc. 4. Holy Spirit. I. Title.
 BS2545.C45 G62 2017   233

Cover design by Jon Ramsey

First Fruits Press

The Academic Open Press of Asbury Theological Seminary

204 N. Lexington Ave., Wilmore, KY 40390

859-858-2236

first.fruits@asburyseminary.edu

asbury.to/firstfruits

ADOPTION

By

W. B. Godbey

AUTHOR OF
'New Testament Commentaries" "New Testament
Translation,"_and a great number of
other books and booklets.

Published by

THE APOSTOLIC MESSENGER OFFICE

900 SILVER RUN AVE.

Greensboro, North Carolina

ADOPTION

Among the financiers of the world, Mr. Hope, the great banker of Holland was exceedingly prominent, in his day recognized as pre-eminent by the whole financial world, and of course accumulating a princely fortune. A young man, very bright and promising was serving him as sexton, who in the providence of God becomes acquainted with the beautiful and charming daughter of Emaphoon of London, England,won her heart and sought her hand in wedlock; her father putting his veto on most positively on account of his poverty, therefore he put his wits to work, to meet the emergency and if possible secure the grand enterprise of his life, therefore he negotiated with the girl to ask her father, if he would not give his consent in the event that he was the partner of Mr. Hope the rich banker, to which he readily, aquiesced. Then he negotiates with Mr. Hope asking him if he would give him a partnership in the bank in case that he was the son-in-law of Mr. Emaphoon, in which he also responded encouragingly. Then he proceeds to manoeuvre the matter, so as to have the transactions simultaneous with the wedlock; all running along in reciprocal harmony satisfying all parties concerned; thus the matrimonial alliance, felicitously consummated, and the partnership entered into simultaneously and satisfactorily. He proves a grand financial success, the years come and go; Mr. Hope superanuates, and he takes his place, he goes on into eternity and this young man succeeds him in the presidency; thus gradually climbing from the broom to throne of the millionaire, one of the richest men in the world. You see this grand financial achievements, as well as matrimonial victory, de-

veloped out of adoption in the banking associa-
tion.

(a)   Quite a while ago I became acquainted with
Rev. M. W. Knapp through the books of his author-
ship, and himself with me through the same medium. When he migrated from Albion, Michigan to
Cincinnati, and eventually launched the institutions on the Mount of Blessings, he said I was the
founder, rather than himself, because in the providence of God, instrumental in his launching the Bible school, publishing house and concomitant institutions. He took into his employment, an exceedingly brilliant damsel Bessie Queen whom he adopted
as a daughter, the normal sequence of her extraordinary sufficiency, as a helper in his editorial work

(b)   When the Lord called him from labor to rest
Rev. M. G. Standley was in his employment, pastor
of a mission in the city, who eventually entered into
wedlock with Bessie Queen; thus on the beautiful
hypothesis of matrimonial unification, both of them
becoming his adopted children. This adoption in
the good providence of God actually brought them
the happy succession of the glorified founder of all
these noble institutions which now shine on this holy mountain, sending their light around the world,
actually the summit of all the sacred mountains,
honored of God at the present day from the rising of
the sun to the going down of the same. God in His
providence has permitted your humble servant in
his peregrinations around the world to visit the Bible
colleges in every land and clime, giving them special attention, as he used his humble instrumentality in founding not a few of them. Thus in his
mercy permitted me to sojourn and encourage them
with my humble service, and enjoy extraordinary
privileges in the way of diagnoses, I find the light
shining brighter and the fire burning hotter on the
Mount of Blessings in Cincinnati than any where

else on terra firma. Whereas the brilliancy, fer-
vor and glory shining out from this mountain, really manifests more gorgeous splendor and perma-
nent fire than elsewhere in all the earth, we must
recognize Sister Ramabai's great Bible school at
Soteria India, by herself cognomened "salvation"
which is the meaning of the Muratic word because
she gives it the absolute pre-eminence. She has all
sorts of factories and institutions, simultaneously
running in order to work her students fifteen hundred girls and three hundred boys, the latter only
to do work peculiar of men, e. g. blacksmith and
other works, demanding muscular power; while she
has all sorts of factories appertaining to clothing
for her people and much merchandise and among
them a publshing house. When I arrived she had
sent to **Cincinnati** for all the books of my author-
ship, so she could proceed to publish them in the
languages of that country. I happen to have a copy
of my N. T. translation with me, which she proceeded at once to publish in the **Murati** language.

(f) While all sorts of manual labor receive the
attention necessary to run the institution, giving
all the students an opportunity to pay their own way
if necessary, fifty acres in gardens, abundantly ir-
rigated by the great well peculiar to that country,
twenty five feet in diameter and the water drawn
up with cattle, which they work instead of horses;
yet as on the sacred mountain, I found the decisive
pre-eminence given to salvation, all the way
through; making the place so hot, that every one
would either take fire or run from the fire, as all
acquainted with the work of the Mount of Blessings will certify; to the honor of the trustees, Sister Knapp, Brother and Sister Standley, nobody
stays here without catching the Pentcostal fire and
keeping it with increasing intensity, the longer they
stay. When I preached there, in an audience of

two thousand (not half so large a crowd as that
number in this country because the Asiastics use
neither benches nor chairs; but all sat gracefully and
correct on the floor, not using half the room necessary with all the furniture, utilized in an American
auditorium, as I always in that country preached
straight and positively on regeneration for every
sinner and sanctification for every Christian, winding up with an invitation to all who did not enjoy
these experiences to come to the altar and seek in-
defatigably till the victory from heaven descended,
which always tells its own story.

   (g) Behold I found an altar of a thousand people.
Then I proceeded definitely to tell them how to get
it; as a Christian's God, unlike the gods of India
who cannot do anything, finds no hard job; I assured them that He would certainly verify His prom-
ises, which I gave them, "Ask and ye shall receive,
seek and ye shall find, knock and it shall be opened
unto you; for he that asketh receiveth, he that seek-
eth findeth and to him that knocketh it shall be
opened. If we ask anything in his name, we know
He hears us, and if we know He hears us, we know
we have the petition asked of Him," throughout
that country in the heathen temples, we see their
gods, round the wall sitting on the pedestals.
When they go into worship them they ring a bell
to wake them up; thinking that they sleep when
there is no worshipper about. So I told them, the
Christian God never does sleep, but I always lis-
tening to hear the voices of any who will seek his
pardoning mercy, saving or sanctifying power; but
he wants to hear your voices. In that country there
are a hundred nations, speaking a hundred different
languages. Now said I, you speak to Him in your
own language (of course I spoke through an inter-
preter, whom they all understood) when I told
them that the Christian's God understood their lan-

guage perfectly and they had nothing to do but to
speak to Him freely as He would to hear their voices,
as He was certain to do all that He had promised,
saving and sanctifying them all, giving them everything that they needed, to the sinner a new heart,
and the Christian a clean heart and to the backslider
a glorious restoration. Then they all took me at
my word, every black, yellow, red and brown mouth
I saw (for there were no white ones) went open and
oh what a roar getting stronger and louder and con-
tinuing on, because I soon found I had an elephant
on my hands as they were proof against all bene-
dictions, holding on all night. As I was running on
the trains constantly, night and day from place to
place (as that country is well supplied with railroads
owned and built by English capitalists, as Briton
has ruled it 160 years; trains running more rapidly
than they do here fifty miles a hour, and I had a
glorious time evangelizing as my fare was only one
third of a cent a mile, with all the accommodation
of a sleeping car, due to philanthropy of Great
Britian in the interest of missions, if I could call
back twenty five years, how I would run all over
that country again, as my American friends would
gladly pay all my railroad expenses.) As it was utterly impossible to adjourn, the congregation, we
continue on all night I of course had to go to bed and
rest my body. At first I was really puzzled and
soliliquized, how can I sleep amid the roar, like
the sound of many waters reminding me of the
ocean billows, leaping the rock bound shore, "my
high nervous temperament will not down and let me
sleep; so I lay on my bed in the prophet's chamber
His beloved sleep" so I respond, "Lord unworthy as
I am I know your love in behalf of your humble servant does super abound; therefore I claim the promise." It is simply wonderful how He put me to
sleep; so I lay on my bed in the prophets chamber

wrapt in ambrosial slumber, resting in the direct embrace of nature's sweet restorer, old somnus, singing lullabies over me and fanning with a profounder slumber so that I dreamed felicitously that I was on the battle field, and pressing the war in the gate of the enemy, exhorting that mighty host of a thousand mourners as in my youthful days, while at the same time I was in the prophet's chamber alone, wrapped in peaceful slumber, in recuperation of my worn and weary body, the more exhausted by reason of that tropical climate. Eventually when the broad day has driven away the dreary night and I rise to take my train, I find **inundations** of joyful news from the battle field; many sinners gloriously saved and shouting the victory, Christians not a few, forded the Jordan and were shouting down the walls of Jerico, also others have received a definite call to preach the everlasting gospel in that dark land where they are so much needed. I can never forget those memorable three months in great India; meanwhile I travelled six thousand miles by rail, and saw more people converted, sanctified and called to preach than ever before in the same length of time.

(j)　Sister Ramibai's work in that country reminded me of the Mount of Blessings in this, as Mount Blanc above the Alps towers above all, so the Bible school of this wonderful native prophetess, of the Braham high caste in that dark land where idolatry has dominated through the long by gone centuries and ages, towers above all the other mountain peaks on which the lights of truth and Holiness are shining, to guide the priest ridden millions to great High Priest eternally living and officiating in the succession of Melchizedec.

(k)　Hence you see as this Bible school in spirituality enjoys the prominence throughout, not only this great new world, but the inhabitable earth, so

in my wide world peregrination I find the people
everywhere turning their faces towards this Holy
mountain and longing to tread its sacred altitudes
and sit at the feet of the sanctified Gamaliels, who
here expound the precious word of the Lord, by
which every son and daughter of Adam's ruined race
is saved, sanctified, panoplied, fed and have the
victory over the world, the flesh, and the devil and
enjoy a heaven in which to go to heaven, the course
of study now really takes in everything necessary in
the collegiate curriculum; the Lord having used my
humble instrumentality the present year to strength-
en it by the valuable accession of God's precious
word in the language in which He and His apostles
preached it. Consequently hence forth all the students will have the wide open door to study His
precious Word in the beautiful rich and heroic
Greek, which God used that nation miraculously to
formulate and thru their champion, Alexander the
great, by his universal conquest, transmit to all nations; so when Jesus and His apostles preach the
gospel in that language it was in that time the clas-
sical tongue of every nation under heaven.

(l) Not only have we in His good providence ad-
ded the Greek scripture to the curriculum, but the
Latin, which through not the original, is of im-
mense value, because it is the oldest translation,
having been made in the Apostolic age, with Apostolic endorsement and circulation. Therefore the
juveniles called of God, to preach the glorious gospel
will henceforth enjoy every desirable facility on this
sacred mountain.

(m) When Brother Knapp was translated to
heaven, as a normal consequence the management
of these great educational and philanthropic institutions devolved on Brother and Sister Standley as
the shock wrought so heavily on the nerves of Sister
Knapp, as to disqualify her to give them much help;

Sister Mary Storey selected by Brother Knapp to assist them in the trusteeship was is a few years also honored by an angelic convoy, leaving the other three alone; the weight of labor and responsibility devolving on Brother and Sister Standley, who by some of the malcontent contributors to the building funds were pronounced too young and consequently in 1906 an effort was made by them to depose them from the trusteeship; bringing the matter into the civil court, charging them with maladministration deserving ejectment from the trusteeship. I was in California when the suit was brought and consequently the prosecution came off in my absence and I was not present in any of the courts; tho the malcontents tried hard to draw me in. As the charges were all made from the standpoint of maladministration, and while I transacted more business with them than any other person in the world I had never seen anything wrong and was consequently utterly incompetent either directly or indirectly to co-operate with the malcontents; but waited patiently till the litigation was all consummated and taken out of court.

(n) Then I took it on myself to visit the presiding judge in his residence, meet him face to face and receive his personal testimony in reference to the prosecutions, when he told me positively that none of the charges were sustained, and consequently the allegations of maladministrations had all proved effete and the court had fully exonerated the accused, finding no valid testimony for their connection

(o) Law suits like "Aesop's Fable" of the two cats, which found a cheese and fought over it mutually making the fur and blood fly all around, when the monkey interposed as a minister of peace; expostulating with them to desist from their mutual affliction either of the other at the same time

offering his service as a peace maker, dividing it
equally between them You know it would be impossible to cut the cheese in two precisely equal
pieces so they would perfectly balance each other.
Therefore when he divided it putting a piece on either end of the scale and the one pulled down the other, he ate off the heavy piece pretentiously to secure
equillebruim thereby meeting his contract to make
an equal division.

(p) So he ate the heavy piece till the other tilted
it up; then going, ate that piece till it tilted up.
Consequently the cats saw that that the course he
was persuing he would simply eat up both pieces and
leave them none and consequently interposed begging him to desist, proposing to the settle it
themselves; when he laconically responded "I am
glad that my service has been so successful in your
mutual pacifications; but the balance of it is due me
for my service," and consequently proceeded to
eat it all. This illustrates the fact that you cannot
afford to go into law because even tho you win, you'll
suffer financially. This proves sadly true in the law
suit against the Mount of Blessings. Tho the charges
were not sustained and really they were winners in
the suit; yet in sundry ways they suffered financially.

(q) It is a consolatary fact that amid all the
clouds and storms, snow blizzards, icebergs, and
flotillas Satan never succeeded in quenching the
pentecostal fire which has wrapped their mountain
from the very beginning; The camp meetings
throughout lugubrious years of litigation never cool-
ing down; but retaining the Pentecostal flame, un-
abated which still continues, hotter, stronger, and
brighter as the years come and go and His glorious
appearing draweth neigh.

(r) Whereas the juniority of Brother and Sister
Standley was really the great allegation; the pendu-

lum is now swinging potently towards the other
pole of the battery, as the holiness people are unit-
ing in prayer to God; to   run   these educational
and philanthropic institutions without a break till
Gabriel blows His trumpet and the glorious coming King catches his waiting bride

CHAPTER ONE

WITNESS OF ADOPTION, ROMAN 8:16

"The Spirit Himself beareth witness   with   our
spirit that we are the children of God. Man is a trinity, as he was created in the   image or likeness
of God, consisting of spirit,   soul   and body; the
latter simply the tenement in which he dwells; the
house of the **psychee,** soul, consisting of the intellect
memory, judgment, sensibilities and   the   physical
life, during our probation, while we are tested and
tried, our virtues matured and graces perfected,
antecedently to the glorious immortality awaiting
the faithful pilgrimage, whereas the body is the
tenement of the **pnunma,** the human spirit.   When
the transfiguration supervenes and this mortal shall
put on immortality.   Or in thought of our probation
expiring antecedently to his   glorious   appearing
so He will send an angel as in case of Lazarus to
call us away, leaving this tenement in the bosom of
mother earth for desintegration till relieved by the
resurrection angel when its veritable identy will
be perpetuated, a spiritual entity, imponderable and
indestructible as a unit cannot undergo disintegration and consequently survives eternally the tenement of the **pneuma,** human spirit in contradis-
tinction to the present probation, meanwhile it is
the house of the **psychee,** the soul.
     (a)   The reason why this body in the grave un-

dergoes disintegration is because like other physical
entities is is composed of the   62   elements which
constitute the constituencies of the earth, oxygen,
hydrogen, nitrogen, sulphur, phospherus, cohon,
calcium, alumnium, gold, silver, iron, copper, etc;
whereas the transition out of the material into the
spiritual will eliminate all the earthly element and
consequently render the body forever imponderable
i. e. will not weigh anything. 'This wonderful transition, out of the material into the spiritual in case
of all who die will be superinduced by the resurrection, in which the same body will be raised from
the dead; but no longer physical having been meta-
morphosed into the spiritual.

(t)   The human spirit consisting of the conscience
the will and the affections is really the man proper;
the mind is grand enduement contradistinguishing
him from the animal creation and the body simply the tenement in which he dwells. Therefore the
plan of salvation appertains directly to the human
spirit, on which the Holy spirit operates; passing
on reaching the **psychee,** the immortal mind or soul
and thru it reached the mortal body,. and thence
coming on into the material world, of which man
was created king and woman queen; Satan having
dethroned them and also inslaved them; yet thru
the wonderful redemption scheme, in the succession
of the ages till the final and glorious restitution;
combinating in Satans' dethronement eternal defeat
and with all his followers demoniacal and human,
ejectment into the lake of fire, in outer darkness,
beyond the illuminated universe so infinitely distant
that the combined luminosity of 217 million suns
will never reach it with a cheering ray; meanwhile
this earth having reached her final Edenic restitution so brilliantly revealed in the last two chapters
of the Bible will be the paradisian abode of humani-

ty, walking with God in the beauty of holiness and glorifying Him thru the flight of eternal ages.

(u)   The conscience is the medium of conviction, as it is God's telephone through which he speaks to the human spirit, the only faculty which survived the fall, snatching away the banner of human hope, from the strong cruel grip of Satan, and planting it on the ramparts of coming generations to wave in thrilling anticipation of the glorious redemption, which God purchased with the gift of His son to pour out His blood on rugged calvary to redeem the lost millions engulfed by the fall in the unfathomable abyss of eternal dispair; thus rescuing every son and daughter of Adam's human race by the Omnipotent grip of Judah's lion. Here we see the awful vortex of the unpardonable sin, committed by the blasphemy of the Holy Ghost, who speaks to the sinner, through the telephone of his conscience, opening his blind eyes to see the lurid flames of an unquenchable hell, coming to meet him, unstop his deaf ears to hear the deep toned thunder of his own damnation coming to greet him, and thus beat the alarm drums sending panic to his guilty soul.

(v)   It is awfully dangerous to turn a deaf ear to the warnings of a guilty conscience. Vice as a monster if so frightful mean, that to be hated, needs but to be seen; but seen too often, we first endure; then pity and embrace. When the prophet Elisha saw Hazael, and looking in his face began weeping because he saw the awful, diabolical cruelties he would inflict on Israel, ruthless murdering, the old, young great and small, even the unborn, and told him so; when he responded, do you think your servat is a dog that he would go such things! Of course he felt outraged at the very thought and could not have been convinced that he would ever be guilty of those diabolical atrocities; yet he went directly to the royal palace, with a lie in his mouth,

telling the King, that the Prophet said he would get
well, when he had already anointed him in his succession. Then watching his opportunity, he put a
thick wet cloth over his face, and held it until he
smothered him to death, took the throne of Syria
and during his reign invaded Israel, with bloody
and cruel wars committing on the people the very
same appalling cruelties, Elisha had predicted when
first mentioned his conscience revolted at the very
thought; yet he went on from bad to worse, till he
torpified his conscience, searing it with the hot
iron of blasphemy and rebellion, till he hushed the
angel voice amid his outrageous demoniacle cruelties, till the angelic warning no longer rang in his
ears; like Burke, the London murderer, made his living by selling human bodies to the surgeons in the
medical colleges for postmortem dissection, killing
them when he could not otherwise procure them;
testifying under the gallows that the first murder
shocked him, almost into paralysis; the next not so
much, and still weakening until he cared no more
to murder a human being than to butcher in the
slaughter pen, slaying the animals for food.

(w) This is the way people seal their doom in
hell; often in their youth so recklessly outraging
the protest of a guilty conscience, as to lull that
guardian angel to sleep, till she never wakes till the
deep tone thunders of damnation peel in, when she
rises, with unprecedented vigor, refreshed by her
long nap, her sister memory by her side, flying by
her side flying back over the track of sinful youth,
hardened manhood and torpified declining years,
gathering up every willful sin, till the pile rises into
a mountain, and though capped with snow symbolic
of the avowed innocency, manipulated by Satan, to
ease the dying hours, till he can precipitate you into
hell; yet the deep toned thunders in the profound
interiors proclaim the accumulated volcanic fires,

which superinduce a cyclone eruption while soul and body part, inundating you with the real burning lake.

(x) While conscience is the medium of conviction the will is the medium of conversation The weakest Christians says yes to the Lord all the time and no to Satan; as one no to God, throws wide open the door of your exodus out of his kingdom into that of Satan. In regeneration, a terrible battle is fought between the Holy Ghost and Satan in which, the former wins the victory, wrestling the will from the devil and turning it over to God. While converted people all say yes to God at every cost; yet many voices anon like croaking frogs and hooting owls, echo and reverberate, from the deep dark jungles, in the quags, precipices, chasms, and deserts of the fallen interior spirit, where still linger, pride, vanity, egotism, selfishness selflove, ambition, coveteousness which is idolatry," lust, passion, temper, hypocricy, guile, malice, animosity, anger, wrath, prejudice, bigotry, jealously, evil appetites, for tobacco, strong drink, opium and diversified narcotics. From this multitude of doleful creatures inhabiting the the dismal dungeons of the fallen human spirit, emanate many a lugubrious no to God, grievious to the Holy Ghost and an awful torment to the regenerated soul, who fights against this diabolical army with all his might or soon goes down under the triumphant tread of their cloven feet to read his doom in lurid capitals on the black walls of the pandemonium; meanwhile cruel myrmidons lash him with fire brands and kick him for a foot ball, around the black walls through the flight of eternal ages.

(y) The remedy for this awful antagonism to the regenerated soul is simply the baptism which Jesus freely gives to all His children, responsively to perfect consecration followed by receptive and appropriative faith; the Holy Spirit the Executive

of the Trinity applying the precious cleansing blood;
thus gloriously expurgating, all this motly host of
stygian imps, perfectly purifying the heart from
all the turpitute of inbred sin and making it the
temple for the abiding comforter, who beautifies us
by his felicitious testimony, bearing witness with
our spirit that we are heaven born and heaven
bound, actually enjoying a heavenly prelibation in
our own hearts; thus not only going to heaven but
taking our heaven with us.

(z) Reader have you this testimony! n. b. you
cannot afford to make this perilous journey without
it. When the Holy Ghost, the Executive of the
Trinity, Convictor of the sinner, Regenerater of the
penitent, Restorer of the backslider, Sanctifier of
the believer and Glorifier of the soul when this mortal shall put on immortality, is knocking at the door
of thy heart and anxious to do His office work, creat-
ing within thee a new heart and putting a new
spirit with in you; thus making you a new creature;
so the material world will all rise before
you in grandeur and more glorious panorama;
the sun, moon and stars shining with more
gorgeous splendor, beauty and glory than ever
before; the mountains and hills more sublimely tow-
ering amid the cerulean vaults of the azure skies
with their snowy pinnacles reflecting the unutterable beauties of the celestial luminaries; the fields
smiling with a fairer green and the gardens with
more charming grandeur and beauty; the oceans,
lakes and rivers revealing the power and glory of
the creative fiat in sublimity, majesty and splendor
hitherto never seen nor heard; till like the little
girl who is seeking the Lord at the altar while the
preacher is in the pulpit dispensing the living Word
when anon she would break out in pitiful moans and
cries and he would throw a hortatory parenthesis
for her personal consolation; when eventually grace

prevails and the victory sweeps down from heaven and leaping to her feet and clapping her hands she says "Glory to God I have got it," and the preacher said "tell us how you got it," oh she said I didn't do anything, i. e. when she quit her own efforts the Lord did it speedily and he says, has the Lord given you a new heart, then she responses "I do not know. but I am sure He has either made me new or made every thing else new because every thing I see looks so beautiful, that it must be brand new.

(a)　When the Lord gives you a new heart he always tells you about it, "the Spirit Himself bearing witness with our spirit that we are the children of God. The same is true in reference to a clean heart he always tells you so in loving confirmation of His wonderful promise, John 1:7, If we walk in the light as He is in the light, the blood of Jesus Christ His Son cleanseth us from all sin, so that we realize inward purity, and hear the bells of heaven ringing from the crown of the head to the soles of the feet, "sanctification holy." Whereas hitherto while your own spirit said yes to God all the time and no to Satan; many voices within faltered in that Yes to God, pride, vanity, ambition, avarice, egotism, envy, jealously, bigotry, prejudice, animosity, hatred, selfishness, self will, sectarianism, politics, lodgery, idolatry i. e. the trend to divide the glory which belongs to Jesus only giving some of it to the water God and other little ecclesiastical idols in counter distinction to the glorious sinking away into his blessed Divinity so deep that Satan will never be able to find you.

(b)　We must reach the similitude of our Saviour's humanity which is our infallable paragon; remembering His words, John 12 when the prince of this world cometh unto me, he findeth nothing in me, i. e. nothing belonging to him. Consequently he always had the real victory, i e. heaven in the heart and in the life. The dearest idol I have known. Whatever that idol be, help me to tear it from thy throne, and worship only thee; so shall my walk be close with God, calm and serene my frame, a light to shine along the road. That leads me to the lamb. Sending up your prayer let me die so dead that no desire shall rise, to pass for good or great or wise, in any but my Saviour's eyes; singing as we go, I am sinking out of self into Christ, thus going down deeper into His blessed divinity. The world constantly receding farther away.

CHAPTER II

THE JOINT HEIR WITH CHRIST, Rom. 8:17

When the elder brother of the prodigal gave way to a degree of iracibility provoked by the vociferous shouts of the people rejoicing over his returned prodigal brother showing His imperative need of entire Sanctification, to take all the fret and jealously out of him; he responded Father I have never at any time transgressed thy commandment, showing he had never lost his infantile justification; but badly needed Sanctification; to take all the fret and jealosy out of Him; "observing to his father,' thou hast neveh so much as given me a kid (a little bit of animal) that I might make merry with my friends, and now that thy son is come who has wasted thy substance in riotous living Thou hast slain for him the fatted calf. Then he responded to him, son thou art always with me and all I have is thine; but it was pertinent that we all rejoice because this thy brother who was lost is found and tho dead is alive again; Thus showing up the fact that every thing God has belongs to his Son Astronomy reveals 217 millions of suns and two billions, 170 million

worlds revolving round them here in our own sys-
tem, Neptune 60 times the magnitude of this
world, Saturn 80 times her magnitude; and Jupiter,
14 times her magnitude, meanwhile, Alcyone of the
Pleiades (seven stars) pronounced by astronomers
12 thousand million times the magnitude of the
earth; of course utterly inconceivable thus beggar-
ing the diagnosis of the Annan intellect to compre-
hend, the unutterable vastitude we do not wonder
that the astronomical world unanimously pronounced Alcyone the primal center of the vast universe, honored to contain the palace of the Great
King, with the thrones of the heavenly heirarchies
around which the 217 million suns accompanied by
their respective retinues by chiding two billions 170
million worlds and now revolving, but this was upset
in 1913, by the discovery of 100 millions suns that
had never before been reached as is shown at Har-
vard University Observatory on the Andes mountains of South America; meanwhile they also dis-
covered that Alcyone is moving, confirming the conclusion that she is not the primal center; and consequently the astronomical world are again at sea,
ranging the fenceless fields of the etherial universe,
with their powerful telescopes laboring to discover
the primal center, honored to contain the throne of
God, and around which all suns with the concomitant worlds and revolving.

(c)   Now turn to Eph. 1st chapter Col. 1st chapter, and we find that our Saviour is the creator of all
these worlds, establishing the conclusion that the
divinity becomes creative in the second person therefore as He created all things innumerable worlds,
pronounced by the greatest astronomers, collective-
ly but the suburbs of the celestial universe; from
the fact that the telescopes all rest on vast fields of
Nebula, so infinitely distant as to be unindividualiza-
ble by the most powerful telescopes   Therefore the

mind is lost in inutterable bewilderment, as we con-
template the vastitude of God's universe. As our
Saviour is His only Son, of course He inherits it all.
What belongs to the King, also belongs to the
Queen; the property of her husband is that of his
wife his better half. The saints constitute the
bridehood of Christ and the Queenship of Heaven.
As the son of God created all of these two billions
and a 170 million worlds, some of which are so wonderfully large, e. g. Alcyone, 12 thousand million
times the magnitude of this earth. We have it
clearly revealed in Eph. 1st chapter and Col. 1st
Chapter that our Saviour created them all; consequently they belong to Him, as the saints constitute
the bride of Christ and whatsoever belongs to Him
also belongs to her; therefore in Him we actually
inherit all things visible and invisible and on earth;
our joint heirship with Him, securing to us everything that belongs to Him.

(d) My arm is identified with my body through
the joint by which it is really a part of my body.
Therefore all the movements which my body received are participated by every member which is
a joint heir to everything belonging to the body.
As Christ God's only son inherits all things belonging to Him, so the saints constituting the bridehood
inherits all things when we suffer out our probation and enter the transfiguration glory, receiving
this same body resurrected in the similitude of His
glorified body which on the mount of transfiguration actually eclipsed the mortal vision of Peter,
James and John, so they found it necessary to cover
their eyes with their hands, as they prostrate lay on
the ground; so this body, will shine in its transfiguration glory, when resurrected in case God should
send an angel to call us away and leave this body for
the interment of our survivors, or in case that He
should come for us while still lingering on these

argillaceous tenements as Paul assures us, we will be transfigured in the twinkling of an eye, I. Cor. 15:51 We shall not all sleep but we shall all be changed, in a moment in a twinkling of an eye, for the mortal shall put an "immortality; this corruption, and mortality shall be swallowed up of life.

(e) In this probation we are all caterpillars eating the green leaves from the cesspools. The very same caterpillar, from which we turn with loathing next year will be the beautiful butterfly on golden pinions winging his flight from one flower to another, only deigning to light on the beautiful rosy petals whence he drinks the honey dews; in his beauty, splendor and angelic similitude, profoundly impressing us of his origin and destination; yet a year ago he was thy loathsome caterpillar, from whose contemplation you turned away with Nausea.

(f) As our glorious Lord created all these two billion 170 million worlds and as astronomers believe even all these reached by telescope observation constitute but the supurbs of the celestial universe; Oh; the incomprehensibility of our wonderful Christ, in His created omnipotents; Bishop Marvin one of the brightest saints who ever walked the earth gives it as his candid opinion that when God takes us away is because he has more use for us in some other world.   ,

(g) The wonderful plan of salvation is for the restoration of this fallen world and the fortification of all others worlds against the liability of falling which proves so fatal to us as to plung us into irretrievable ruin, if God had not reached down His omnipotent arm, of redeeming grace and dying love, thus lifting us, from the depts of hell to the heights of heaven, to wear a starry crown and play on a golden harp while the cycles of eternity speed their precipited flight. As this is the only fallen world

of which we have any information; doubtless our
great work, through the oncoming fugitive ages
will be the fortification of the newly created inhab-
itants of these infinitesimal worlds against aposta-
sy, and who would be so efficient preachers as we
people who have passed through Satan's flint mills,
again and again, coming out with a shout of victory
every time, rest assured we can beat the angels
out of sight as they have never known, sin nor
sorrow; just as the most efficient slum workers in
the rescue of dissapation, debautchery, drunkenness,
groveling sentualities; and misery actually suffer
hell torment in lugubrious prelude ; for excelling
those who like your humble servant never suffered
the crushing torture superinduced by wreched hab-
its.

(h)   Oh! the incomprehensible glory awaiting us
in the realms of the blessed when we shall wing our
flight from world to world, with adoring wonder,
contemplating, the stupendous works of any omnipotent creator, and how unutterable delightful to
preach the gospel of divine loyalty to the fallen angels who have never known sin nor sorrow. As
we will be immortal, we can prosecute enterprises,
comprehending thousands of years, as we will know
that we are immortal and consequently live forever.

(i)   What a wonderful evangelistic field will we
find the planet Jupiter, which is 14 hundred times
the size of this world. Therefore we can deliberately
move out on an evangelistic tour, actually requiring
a thousand years, 10 thousand or a million, Oh! the
unutterable glory of joint heirship with the son of
God. What a wonderful inspiration, to us all, to
be perfectly submissive joyfully obedient and de-
lightfully loyal to our blessed heavenly Father. The
very thought of living coeternal with God and doing

His will like the unfallen angels around the effulgent
throne, should raise us on tiptoe and flood us with
holy gratitude till we actually constantly behold
a transcendently glorious panorama of winging our
flight through trackless either with lightening ve-
locity Luke 10:18, from world to world, exploring
God's wonderful and boundless universe, leaping over milky waves, and soaring above the long fiery tails
of the wondering comets, meanwhile we will enjoy
the delightful privilege of co-operating with our
Blessed Savior, in His glorious administration of
love, wisdom, righteousness and holiness, through
the flight of eternal ages.

THE CONSANGUINITY OF THE HOLY GHOST

From my earliest childhood, I was wonderfully
fond of my kinfolks, so glad for them to come and
see us; thinking them far better than any other
people in the world, of course because they talked
to me kindly, manifesting a great interest in me
and of course eulogizing me as I was exceedingly
susceptible, and proficient in everything I undertook
in study, excelling and receiving commendation
from everybody.   In the schools, they only taught
the spelling book the readers, elementary arithme-
tic and writing.   I excelled in them all, learning
the spelling book by memory, so that I actually
could spell everything in it.   They often had spelling
matches, in which I always excelled all my com-
rades, the last day of school was always a time of
great interest; the people crowding in to hear the
children spell by memory as that was the only ex-
amination exercises they had.   On the occasion, a
neighbor school all adjourned to attend our closing
day and beat us all spell as that was the only schol-

arship that was brought before the public. They always began with the spelling book and went through it, starting off with the monosyllable going on to dissyllables, then trisyllables, followed by polysyllables indefinitely finally winding up on the losing paragraph which was somewhat like a dictionary, not only spelling the words but defining them.

(j) When that school arrived and challenged us all for a spelling match beginning with little ones and going up to the full grown students; our teacher called me out to begin, starting off with the monosyllables, when I turned down all the primaries, in their school and of course every student stood until he failed to spell something and would consequently be turned down; thus beginning with the youngest, I turned all them down, the older and higher grades coming on, sharing the same fate and all going down, till finally the grown students were on hand and the teacher could go out into the larger and more difficult words as the higher grades came on, till the whole school, went down one by one, finally reaching the last scholar of all, the oldest and regarded as the most proficient, Johnas Measles, who came out full of egotism and thinking he was certain to turn down that little boy, only weighing sixty five pounds, when the teacher gave out to him, "dun, to ask for money" and he spelt it all right; then he gave out to me "dun, a brown color which I spelt, and then to that herculean young man, he gave on "done, performed," and with a stentorian voice he roared out "dun," and I without waiting for the teacher to give it to me, as I knew he had missed it, just spelled it "done" performed which wound up the whole school turned down by the one little boy, when they all shouted uproariously, picked me up and carried me round tossing me in the air, to the infinite delectation of the large crowd, assembled to witness the spelling match between the two schools, and our teacher made most of his victory, just stating to them that he had lots of others like me, if they wanted to try this fight over again.

(k) When in the providence of God I was wedded to my good wife fifty five years ago, at the age of twenty seven, I loved her so much better than myself, that while I did not appreciate her more than mine; thus in one auspicious hour, memorialized in the matrimonial solemnization, I doubted my consanguinity and with great delight preceeded to visit them and rejoice with them in delightful affinities superinduced by the Lord, gracious and merciful institution of holy wedlock.

(l) Eight years subsequently to this matrimonial epoch in my life, the Lord in his wonderful mercy, permitted me to cross the flooded Jordan, into the land of corn and wine, flowing with milk and honey, and superabounding in all the delicous fruits of Canaan; opening the heroic graces of the Christian warrior in the conquest of land under the leadership of our noble Joshua, a Hebrew word which means Jesus, thus superinducing the thrilling campaigns which proved so delightful to my warriors spirit, especially the great culminating victory of Bethhoran, so gloriously commemorated by the halting of the king of day, holding still the fiery wheel of his solar chariot over Gibean; meanwhile the moon stopped all the glittering beauty of her queenly chariot, over the valley of Aijelon till Joshua could finish his battle; thirty one kings, representing all south Canaan, combined against him, feeling that perfectly sure of victory; but all losing their crowns, scepters and thrones, doffed submissively at Joshua's feet.

(m) Now we go for the great north and meet the confederated Boreal armies, under the command

of Jabin the King of Asor, at the water of Merom,
where we see another brilliant victory gloriously
perch on Joshua's banner, when they all go down in
blood and so crimson Lake Merom as to give him the
aspect of a bloody sea, when our triumphant captain
calls us all to a great national conversion at Shiloh,
where He gives us all our inheritance, a rich farm
we have never cleared, magnificent mansions, we
never built, prolific orchards we never planted, sup-
erabouding vineyards burdening the earth, with
their delicious grapes which we had never planted
or pruned.

(n) Amid these wonderful and unprecedented in-
vironment, so vividly contrasting the lugubrious
peregrinations of forty years in the wilderness,
chased by the Amalekites, from pillar to post; so
signally defeating us, that we actually marched to-
ward the Red Sea, till halted by Moses and Aaron
and their prophetess sister Miriam, Joshua and Ca-
leb in a rousing campmeeting, till reclaiming grace
and converting power descending from heaven in
showers of blessing; superinducing a right about
face, turning us back to fight our way through and
reach the promised land, or bleach our bones on the
battlefield. Not only while a slave toiling in the
brick fields and mortar yards of Egypt, but during
my wilderness peregrination, which lasted nineteen
years, as there were no holiness people to tell me
how to get sanctified; because I never heard a ser-
mon on it, till after the Lord gave me the experience
forty-seven years ago; as I shall always believe if
I had not been caught by the water god when I con-
strained the Methodist preacher to immerse me as
others had told me if I went under the water I
would get the victory; but finding it a sad mistake
as old Adam, like his cousins the snake and the frog,
could live in the bottom of the creek as well as on
the mountain pinnacle; even so I found him to tena-

cious of life for me to drown him, and hence the change only from dry to wet, the wilderness howl still resounding amid the mountain crags and desert wastes, more lugubriously than ever before, and so continued, till I finally lost sight of the water god, when he retreated before the coming fiery cyclone, finding a hiding place in a great fog bank, so I lost sight of him forever, till his ingress into my experience seems like a dream, fugitive contemporaneously with the night watch, till like that of Nebuchadnezzar it actually evanesced till it seems as if it had never been.

(o) During my Egyptian slavery and wilderness fraternities of consanguinity, affinity and their normal auxiliaries, lodgery, in which I found sunshine and happiness which I was always ready to recognize and appreciate as bright and blooming oasis in the howling wilderness through which I beat my marches, bound for the promise land. Moses was a powerful preacher on sanctification. He did not talk to the toiling slaves in Egyptian bondage about the howling wilderness through which they had to pass, but eloquently spread before them a brilliant panorama of the land of Canaan, flowing with milk and honey and abounding with wine, till their mouth watered and they longed to be there.

(p) The great reason why Moses could not reach the promised land, was because he was their legislator in the providence of God and it would have encouraged the dangerous heresy that we can get sanctified by good works which is now the doctrine of the great Catholic Church, deluding 450 millions We admit that he backslid at the waters of Meribah, when he imbibed impatience but soon got reclaimed. Great truth underlies the literal revelation of the Bible as in this case his identity with the law, rendered it unsafe for us as we are prone to look to our own good works to sanctify us, which is simply a stratagem of Satan to keep us from getting it.

(q) Aaron had to die in the wilderness as you see he was buried on Mt. Horeb, as Moses on Pisgah and never permitted to reach the promised land, because he was the high priest, and it would have encouraged people to depend on bishops, presiding elders, pastors and churchisms to sanctify them and thus Satan would cheat them out of the blessing without which no one shall see the Lord.

In a similar manner, Miriam must die in the wilderness, because she was a flaming holiness evangelist, and her ingress into Canaan would have encouraged the heresy to which the people have an almost incorrigible predilection, i.e., to depend on the holiness evangelist to sanctify them, an awful heresy, consanguinous to that of looking to the Catholic priest, the Campbellite preacher and the Mormon prophet, turning you over to the water god, weak as water and as grossly idolatrous as the pagan gods of wood and stone. I had to get away from them all, till they all evanesced, immersion lingering longer than any other, but finally retreating into a fog bank and thus disappearing never again to be seen; leaving me in a large place, when I saw Jesus only, when something happened which beggars the vocabulary of the hundred thousand English words to reveal. He baptized me with the Holy Ghost and fire, burning up the Free Mason, the Odd Fellow (I was chaplain in both lodges, attending the meetings every week, serving as their preacher) also the college president, where my conscience had put me, and the Southern Methodist preacher which I had inherited from my father, and the fog bank into which the water god had retreated; giving me the shine, the shout and the leap, which has been growing on me these forty seven years, now at the age of eighty two keeping me in

the vigor of my manhood, so I do more preaching
than my gospel sons in their youth, all around me.

Oh, the blessing and the power, that the Lord
    gave me then
  I never shall forget!
Even now it's stealing over me again and again,
  It lingers with me yet.
For I never shall forget how the fire fell
  When the Lord sanctified me;

Thus radically revolutionizing me not only spirit-
ually, intellectually, physically, socially, but consan-
guinously; thus verifying our Savior's wonderful
promise that those who leave houses, lands, father,
mother, husband, wife, children, friends, neighbors
and kindred for the kingdom of God shall receive
one hundred fold in this life, i. e., one hundred to one
on all of these lines of social and consanguinous re-
lationship, domestic, ecclesiastical, political, educational, and every other way, and in the life to come
life everlasting.   I have found it verily true, in all
these diversified ramifications; people begging me
everywhere to go to their homes and take a rest.

(s) In my youth my mind reached out for traveling as I was always an insatiable lover of know-
ledge, in whose acquisition traveling is an exceedingly prolific facility; but as I never had money,
which is indispensable to grease carwheels, and buy
ocean steamer tickets, and really demanded every
step we take in our peregrinations around the world;
how I was surprised 22 years ago when expounding
the blessed Bible in the original Greek, in the largest
campmeeting in the world, Waco, Texas, with 4000
tenters and 20,000 people, a man shouted out from
the audience, "Brother Godbey, why do you not
write the commentaries? We are afraid you will
die and we will never get them." I respond, "I must

visit the Holy Land before I do that as the Land and the Book are so intimately associated that I can not write up one without the other and he responded, "Why do you not go?" When I answered, " I lack the finances." At the close of the lesson, a man who did not look like he was worth $500, J. L, Hinton, walked out from the audience and said to me, "Brother Godbey, I have $1500, lying in the bank and no special use for it; the Lord tells me to give it to you to go to the Holy Land." Consequently I was soon sailing on the great waters. Thus He used that man to augment my circuit by the accession of the Old world to the new and I have subsequently made the four journeys and would now be on the waters, were it not for the oriental war.

(t) The same man now lives in California; that land of perennial summer, where the flowers never fade and the fruits never fail. He lives in a house of many mansions and is said to be worth $100,000. As I peregrainate the continent I always stop with him; really dreading to meet him because he begs me so hard to quit work, take my good old better half, who has seen 75 years walking with me 55 and has the fortune to enjoy the acquaintance of this noble friend of ours who has eaten at our table. He begs me hard to take her and come to his house, take choice of rooms from cellar to garret, all we want, more in and be at home till the trumpet blows and at the same time charging me to bring no money, assuring me that every bill is paid. Of course I must go and preach so long as the Lord lets me have the trumpet, I must blow it, till the golden harp comes in sight. He is only one of the many on that same line, thus illustrating the verification of our Savior's promise that if we forsake house and home for his kingdom he will give us 1000 fold in this life and in the world to come life eternal.

Years ago while reading Cicero the greatest Roman orator in the world in his day, I struck the sentence, "Simillibus similes congreganter, birds of a feather flock together. He quotes it as a trite maxim which doubtless came down from the first generation on the earth as it seems to have such antiquity. Rest assured it has a wonderful significance in its pertinency verified in every country under heaven.

(w) In my peregrinations through all lands, I simply go to the holiness people regardless of cognomen, race or color; as they are my people and I feel at home with them as with no others.

www.ingramcontent.com/pod-product-compliance
Lightning Source LLC
Chambersburg PA
CBHW030312030426
42337CB00012B/688